PARENTING A GIFTED CHILD

Understand giftedness and help
your child to thrive

Written by Aurélie Dorchy
In collaboration with Antonella Delli Gatti
Translated by Rebecca Neal

Health and Wellbeing   50MINUTES.com

PARENTING A GIFTED CHILD

UNDERSTAND YOUR CHILD AND HELP THEM THRIVE

- **Problem:** it is tempting to think that having a gifted child will make your life easier, but often this could not be further from the truth. With this in mind, how can you resolve the range of problems facing gifted children and those around them?
- **Aims:** to understand giftedness in order to support your gifted child at home and at school so that they can make the most of their talents.
- **FAQs:**
  - What are the steps to getting my child officially classified as gifted?
  - What teaching methods and alternatives to school are there for gifted children?
  - What are the signs that a child has high intellectual potential?
  - Does my child absolutely require psycholo-

gical support?
- Are the parents and siblings of a gifted child necessarily gifted as well?
- Should I be worried if my child only socialises with other gifted children?
- Are gifted individuals more at risk of depression?

The term "gifted" refers to individuals whose intellectual abilities are far above the norm, although there is no single fixed definition of giftedness and definitions of the phenomenon vary between cultures.

Whatever definition is used, gifted children often struggle with the fact that some people expect them to be an all-knowing genius because of their abilities, in line with common preconceptions and images in the media and some films (*A Beautiful Mind*, 2001; *Pawn Sacrifice*, 2014; *The Tournament*, 2015).

However, the reality is far more nuanced than this simplistic assumption. Giftedness is much more than an IQ (intelligence quotient) of above 130: it is also a range of emotional and behavioural traits that set gifted children apart from their peers. Gifted children tend to feel more intensely and work differently, which can have a significant effect on all aspects of their lives, not least on their relationships with others.

If you think that your child might be gifted, or if they have already been classified as gifted, you probably have a lot of questions or are unsure how best to support their education.

The challenges of raising a gifted child include answering their existential questions, finding a school that can accommodate their particular needs, dealing with the fear of being seen as arrogant or pretentious by other parents, and handling jealousy from their siblings.

Learning more about giftedness and the tools at your disposal will enable you to tailor your child's education to their abilities and provide them with the best possible guidance throughout their childhood and teenage years. This will allow them to feel supported, fit in with their peers and make the most of their potential.

WHAT IS GIFTEDNESS?

A SERIES OF DIFFERENCES

While every child is different, with their own personality, favourite games and struggles, so-called "gifted" children have a number of distinctive characteristics that you should be able to observe in your child. In this section, we will examine these characteristics.

If you believe that your child may be gifted and they display at least three of the following characteristics, you should look into the matter further. However, you should exercise caution when analysing these indicators, as the presence of one of them does not necessarily mean that your child is gifted.

With very young gifted children, parents will often get the impression that they are struggling to keep up with their child rather than the other way around. The child will frequently try to direct their parents' attention to their surroundings by asking questions that may seem disconcerting for their age.

Gifted children tend to be drawn to many different activities and switch between them rapidly, not because they have a short attention span but because they want to explore and because of their particular way of thinking: one idea quickly leads to another and they make connections that not everyone can see. They are very lively and observant and have trouble sleeping. They typically start talking very early (or at a later age than usual, but at a high level) and walking earlier than the average age (specifically, they may start walking at around a year old and talking before the age of two).

Later on, the intensity of your child's emotions and the level of sensory stimulation they experience may be surprising to you. For example, a gifted child may find sounds that other people consider normal to be too loud. They are also likely to notice more details and try much harder to understand their surroundings by touching objects or memorising smells that other people miss.

Their senses are so acute that they may hate the

feeling of certain materials. Furthermore, situations that seem perfectly normal to you may be much more challenging for your child, who feels things more intensely than their peers, and they may seem to overreact to minor issues, such as a smell that is bothering them or a piece of clothing that is too tight. However, this is simply because gifted children tend to experience a lot of strong emotions.

You may also have noticed that your child is very empathetic and has a keen sense of fairness. Somewhat more uncomfortably, they may pepper you with existential questions that you would rather avoid answering.

Gifted children are quick to learn new things and develop a wide vocabulary at a young age. They tend to be very curious, take an interest in a wide range of subjects at the same time and think very quickly. One of the hallmarks of gifted children is that they can answer questions, but cannot explain the thought process they used to arrive at their answer, so it is clear that they are predominantly guided by their intuition.

Another specific feature of gifted children is

their nonlinear way of thinking. But what does this mean? Most people's thoughts follow on from each other in a logical progression, but nonlinear thinkers follow analogical reasoning. In practice, this means that when a gifted child is thinking, they move rapidly from one subject to another based on an element of comparison, a similarity or a relationship, no matter how tenuous, between different objects or concepts, which means that they can end up a long way from the thing they were thinking about to start with. Furthermore, several different ideas can come to them spontaneously and at the same time, with one idea inspiring a whole series of related ideas, and it may be difficult for others to see the links between them.

These two different ways of thinking can be seen in the diagrams below.

- The first diagram allows us to visualise a "normal" thought process. A person thinks about the fact that they need to find someone to look after their dog. They then search directly for a solution and think about what they should do.

> Who can watch my dog?

↓

Maybe my neighbour will watch him for me.

↓

I will call her at around 4pm.

- The second diagram represents nonlinear thinking. The initial question is the same as in the first diagram but, by a process of analogy, it inspires a range of other thoughts that appear at the same time. The thoughts develop in all directions, but there is always a link to the original question, although this link will not necessarily be immediately clear.

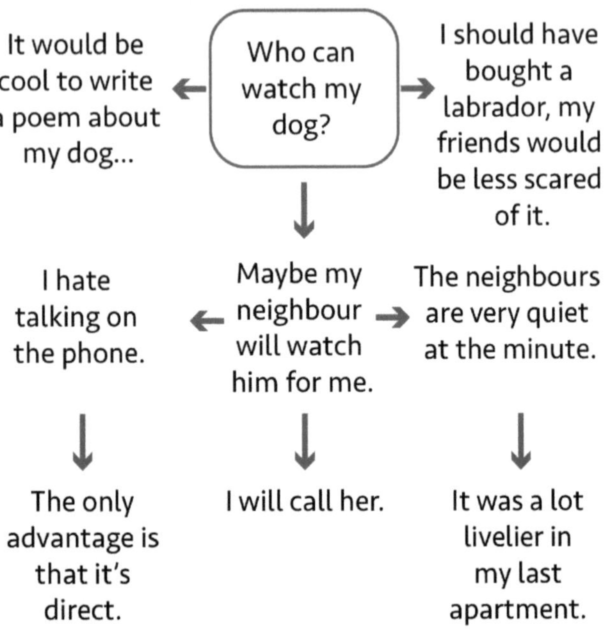

As you may have found out for yourself, gifted children can be difficult to keep up with! As well as thinking in a particular way, they may also feel that they are out of sync with their peers and constantly try to adapt to the people around them.

When other people are surprised by their way of

reasoning or the fact that their attention seems to be focused in a hundred directions at once, they often end up having to explain how they think, but they may struggle to articulate this. The constant need to explain themselves can be exhausting, and this can make it harder for them to fit in with their peers. This means that gifted children often prefer to socialise with older people, for example by talking to teachers during playtime. They may not feel that they belong until they meet other gifted children.

Of course, although gifted children share many of the characteristics we have outlined in this section, they are still all individuals with their own personality, tastes and experiences.

THE IMPORTANCE OF CONFIRMATION

Recognition

Even if your child shows clear signs of being gifted, you may still be hesitant to get confirmation from a specialist. This is understandable, and there are many possible reasons for it: you may be afraid that people will think you are overestimating your own child's abilities; your partner may not take your concerns seriously; you may worry that you will change your child's life for the worse and leave them at risk of being bullied by their peers; or people you know may have had bad experiences getting their child confirmed as gifted.

However, getting confirmation that your child is gifted will help them to understand themselves better, put their everyday experiences into words and manage their giftedness more easily. The knowledge that other people understand what they are going through will often soothe any tension they may be feeling. Conversely, a gifted child who is never officially classified as such may spend years questioning their identity and develop anxiety or depression, as they will not have learned how to deal with the feeling that they do not fit in with everyone else.

> "I've always felt that I didn't fit in with other people, but I never dared to get official confirmation. I was afraid that it would turn out that I wasn't gifted and that I'd been wrong. In addition, I couldn't talk to other people about it, because they might not have understood

why I wanted to be labelled gifted. Finally, some friends, who I think might be gifted themselves, convinced me to take the plunge. Taking the test was a huge relief, and it helped me a lot to know that my experiences had a name and that I didn't need to change who I am to be normal. Now, I wish I'd taken the test when I was a child." (Emily, 54)

Getting confirmation

The only way to get real confirmation that your child is gifted is to work with a specialised psychologist. Having a hunch is not enough, nor is a free IQ test from the internet, as this could lead to inaccurate results and support that is not adapted to your child's needs.

The specialist will do much more than asking the questions that commonly appear in popular IQ tests; they will carry out a comprehensive analysis of your child's mental processes through psychometric and personality tests and by observing their attitude as they respond to the questions.

The IQ test that is commonly used to confirm

giftedness (along with other measures) was developed by the psychologist David Wechsler (1896-1981) in the late 1930s. There are several different versions of it, depending on the patient's age, as an individual's knowledge base will change a great deal between early childhood and later stages of development. The minimum IQ needed to be considered gifted is 130, while also taking into account other elements that the specialist will identify during their psychological assessments.

It is also worth pointing out that the way the child is feeling when they take the test can influence its results, and the psychologist supervising them will take this into account. Furthermore, this test does not measure other kinds of intelligence, and a lower IQ score does not mean that your child is "stupid" or "slow".

Once it has been confirmed that your child is gifted, you will be better able to understand what this means for them, and it will be easier to adapt their everyday environment to their specific needs. The psychologist is there to help you, and they can help you to implement strategies to make the most of your child's strengths and weakness and adapt the education they receive.

SOCIOCULTURAL REPRESENTATIONS OF GIFTED CHILDREN

Giftedness and the particular traits that come with it can inspire strong feelings, and are surrounded by myths and misconceptions. Our perception of this subject is influenced by the way it is presented in our culture, and while this can sometimes help us to grasp what giftedness is, some preconceptions make it harder to understand gifted children.

Common myths about gifted children

Not only do gifted children have to adapt to the world around them, they also have to deal with hard-to-dispel myths about themselves and their parents.

Many people conflate "gifted" with "genius" and cannot understand how a gifted child can fail a test. However, it is now accepted that a third of gifted children will be confronted with failure (see 'Potential difficulties at school').

It is also commonly believed that the parents of gifted children are pushy and put pressure on their offspring. While this may be true of some parents, who have exceptionally high expectations for their children, this is by no means always the case, nor is it limited to the parents of gifted children. That said, the particular needs of gifted children generally mean that their parents will make an effort to help them adapt to society and be happy as they are, which in turn means that they often have to take a more active role in their education and try to ensure that their child works to succeed.

Parents may also have difficulty in their relationships with others because of the jealousy that giftedness can inspire. For example, the parents of gifted children may be accused of being ambitious, having more money or always pushing their child to be better at everything.

These persistent myths help to explain why parents are often hesitant to tell other people that their child is gifted, as they are worried that this may be interpreted as arrogance or pushiness. They may avoid seeking official confirmation, talking to their child's headteacher or even discussing the subject at home.

Furthermore, contrary to popular belief, gifted children still need adult support. A high IQ and early development in some areas does not mean that they are emotionally mature or capable of managing their feelings. As the parent or teacher of a gifted child, you should be there for them and help them to thrive both at school and in their everyday life.

Gifted individuals in film and literature

Gifted and otherwise atypical individuals regularly feature in films, although they are often depicted as high-performing geniuses in particular areas, such as mathematics or chess. This can be seen in films such as *The Tournament*, directed by Élodie Namer (French director and screenwriter, born in 1978), which centres on an incredibly talented chess player.

In a number of films, gifted individuals are recruited by powerful institutions to carry out dangerous missions. For example, in the 1998 film *Mercury Rising* by the American director and producer Harold Becker (born in 1928), a 9-year-old autistic boy is placed under FBI protection because he was able to crack an NSA code and the creator of the code, a man named Krudow, wants to eliminate him to protect his code.

These films are often based on stereotypes about gifted individuals, and their depictions may bear little resemblance to reality. That said, some of them do a good job of representing some of the less obvious aspects of giftedness: the sense of not fitting in, isolation, intuition, a pronounced interest in particular subjects, and the issue of performance.

Your children may enjoy *Vitus* (2006) by Fredi M. Murer (Swiss director, actor and screenwriter, born in 1940), *Little Man Tate* (1991), directed by Jodie Foster (American actress, director and producer, born in 1962), or, more recently, *The Young and Prodigious T.S. Spivet* (2013) by Jean-Pierre Jeunet (French director and screenwriter, born in 1953).

These films show the impact that gifted children can have on those around them thanks to their personality and the particular relationships that they have with other children and adults. They therefore make good family viewing, as they may help you to understand your child better and can introduce your child to characters like them that they can identify with.

The theme of giftedness also appears in other media, such as books and comic strips. For example, the comic book character Mafalda, created by the Argentinian cartoonist Quino (born in 1932), is a young girl who is constantly asking existential questions that unsettle her parents, as they are absorbed in their everyday occupations and are not expecting their daughter's musings. One of the best-known books featuring a gifted child is *Matilda* by Roald Dahl (British novelist, 1916-1990), whose eponymous protagonist is a precocious child and voracious reader who is misunderstood and neglected by her parents.

The table below contains books and films that you can enjoy with your child, and you can add to it as you discover more.

Films	Comic book
• *Vitus* • *Little Man Tate* • *The Young and Prodigious T.S. Spivet*	• *Mafalda*
Children's or young adult books	**Other books**
• *Matilda*, Roald Dahl • *The Curious Incident of the Dog in the Night-Time*, Mark Haddon	• *Louis Lambert*, Honoré de Balzac • *The Solitude of Prime Numbers*, Paolo Giordano • *Flowers for Algernon*, Daniel Keyes • *School Blues*, Daniel Pennac

Ask your child what they think about the characters, whether they identify with them or not, and why they feel that way. This is a great opportunity for you to get to know them better without judgement and for them to express their feelings.

POTENTIAL DIFFICULTIES AT SCHOOL

Being gifted is easier for some people than others. While some make the most of their talents and are able to thrive, others find the effort of adapting on a daily basis overwhelming. For example, gifted children may end up feeling misunderstood and alone because their education is not adapted to their needs and they struggle to connect with other children their age, whereas others feel entirely at home in their surroundings.

Of course, "gifted" is not a one-size-fits-all label: like everyone else, your child has their own personality, temperament and difficulties in particular situations, which depend on the context they find themselves in.

Some gifted children struggle with the fact that they are different from their classmates, and may have been made fun of or labelled a "teacher's pet" for contributing too much in class.

Unsurprisingly, some gifted children end up withdrawing into themselves, and this is especially the case during secondary school when they reach the difficult teenage years. They may self-sabotage and try to blend in with everyone else to stop people from realising that they are different. This is known as intellectual inhibition, meaning that the child does not develop their potential, preferring to act like everyone else and avoid standing out.

As a result, they do not push themselves and may even end up failing at school. Their giftedness will not be self-evident, and you may be afraid that nobody will believe you if you tell them that they are. However, if your child was born gifted, you can be certain that they still are.

Being different from other people in any way is always hard, and gifted children are no exception to this rule. This can make them more sensitive, which explains why gifted children are frequently affected by mood disorders such as depression.

Gifted children can also be anxious by nature, especially given that they are prone to existential questioning and may experience very intense feelings. From a very early age, they may have difficulty sleeping, experience physical discomfort such as itching and have trouble eating.

The fact that they find it difficult to connect with the people around them can result in either isolation or aggression. This aggression does not appear overnight, but develops gradually, as the child constantly feels different and misunderstood and is not allowed to express their legitimate feelings in a school system that is ill-suited to their needs. They have to put effort into managing their emotions, which are often very acute due to their hypersensitive nature, every single day, and may end up getting frustrated and lashing out.

In some cases, this emotional turmoil can result in aggressive behaviour, and the child may display hostility towards an environment that they blame for their difference or their boredom at school. In these cases, aggressive behaviour may be an outlet for the frustration that has been building up in them.

> "Some gifted children in multi-age classrooms [classes in which more than one year group is taught together] are quick to take an interest in what is happening in the year above and are already capable of answering the teacher's questions. They are quick to grasp things and learn faster than other students. In terms of behaviour, some gifted children can be quite disruptive, because they find the work too easy. Furthermore, because it does not take them long to understand things, they can work quickly without making mistakes and finish the tasks they are given early. A lot of things seem obvious to them." (Alice, 24)

It is worth mentioning that some gifted children also have developmental disorders such as autism or disabilities such as deafness. In these cases, mental health support from a professional is essential.

SUPPORTING A GIFTED CHILD

Parenting a gifted child is like parenting any other child, although there are some specific features of gifted children that merit particular consideration. In this section, we will examine three areas that you should pay extra attention to.

INTELLECTUAL FULFILMENT

Helping a gifted child to make the most of their intellectual potential is not always easy.

You may have many questions about your child's education: should they skip a year at school? Should you send them to a specialised school? Are there any methods that can help gifted children to learn?

Skipping a year at school

Once it has been confirmed that your child is gifted, suggesting that they skip a year at school may seem like an obvious first step. If you want to try this, it is best to do it early on in their schooling. You will need to get in touch with their teachers, explain the situation to them and come to an agreement about the best way to proceed.

Make sure that you do not push the teachers too hard, especially if they have limited experience dealing with gifted children. Ask them if they have noticed anything in particular about your child and whether they have any suggestions to help them fit in with their classmates. If they seem prepared to listen, describe some of your child's specific traits, discuss their behaviour at home and talk about how they feel about school. This will allow teachers to adapt their explanations and classwork to your child's needs.

If your child is allowed to move up a year, do not assume that it will all be plain sailing from now on, as they will undoubtedly need your help to get used to all the new faces and their new subjects. Make sure you ask them about their feelings about moving up a year, as they may prefer to stay with their current classmates rather than adapting to the year above them. Remember, every situation is different!

If the school cannot adapt to your child's needs, then they will have to adapt to the school, or they risk feeling shut out. This is something you will have to consider if your discussions with the teaching staff go nowhere. In this case, you will need to talk to your child more on a day-to-day basis to find out how they feel about school and think about possible changes that could be made at home or elsewhere to allow them to thrive.

Another potential solution is to look for a more understanding school which offers adapted teaching and additional work that can motivate your child and allow them to thrive. This does not necessarily have to be a specialised school, as these are few and far between, and other strategies are possible.

Specifically, do not hesitate to get in touch with the school before enrolling your child to ask whether they have adapted teaching for gifted children, look at their website, get in touch with other families who are in the same boat, and ask for information about specialised schools, as these differ between countries.

The value of hard work

Skipping a year at school may help your child in some ways, but it will not solve all their problems, as there will always be the risk that they will be bored at school.

It is absolutely vital to make sure that your child does not neglect their schoolwork and stop putting effort into their homework and revision. It is important that they stay motivated and learn to value hard work, as this will prepare them for more advanced studies. Gifted children often end up resting on their laurels and believing that they will always be able to get by in class without making an effort. They may get top grades without studying some of the time, but this will not always be the case. Furthermore, they may dislike certain forms of learning, such as rote memorisation, and refuse to practise them even though they are required at school or university.

Although your child may find it tedious to learn things by heart, as this does not feed their curiosity, you can explain to them that repetition will strengthen their long-term memory. Give them a precise timeframe in which they need to work hard, for example by setting up a calm, pleasant place to work and suggesting that they work for 50 minutes, or even two 25-minute sessions with a ten-minute break so that they can maintain their concentration. Be firm and show them that you make the rules, and briefly explain why you want them to work hard.

If you notice that, for example, memorisation is the exercise that your child finds the most boring, try introducing them to more fun ways of learning such as simple mnemonic techniques. You could suggest associating each word they have to remember with a colour or a gesture, or sign them up for online exercises.

- **Anecdotes.** Associating a piece of information with a personal or an invented anecdote can be an effective way of remembering it. For example, to remember Henry VIII's six wives, keep their names and wedding dates the same, but add imaginary facts about them: Catherine of Aragon (married in 1509) had a pet cat, Anne Boleyn (married in 1536) liked to go bowling, and so on. You can also invent imaginary situations or come up with rhymes.
- **Movement.** Linking a movement (hand or arm

movements, a dance, etc.) to a piece of information will make it come alive and help your child to remember it.

- **Colour.** This is particularly effective for individuals with synaesthesia (meaning that they naturally associate letters with colours, numbers with sounds, and so on). Feel free to assign colours to concepts, depending on your child.
- **Humour.** Make jokes based on their lessons by using impressions, puns, irony, etc.
- **Image associations.** Make the most of their analogical thinking by associating interesting images with more abstract concepts. For example, you could explain photosynthesis by representing it with a coffee filter that absorbs water, solar panels which receive sunlight, lungs which fill with air, liquid going through a straw (sap), and so on.

Once the child has grasped the idea behind these tools, they can use them by themselves. If they seem unsure how to tackle a particular subject, you can remind them of some tips and set them off on the right track. It all depends on your child: some children can cope by themselves once things have been explained to them, while others need more support and encouragement.

Mental management

If your child is falling behind at school, struggling to remember the things they are taught, stumbling over skills they should have mastered and repeatedly getting bad grades in certain subjects, you may be unsure how to help them. Even worse, you may find yourself getting frustrated at them because you know that they are bright enough to do better.

Mental management, a method developed by the French educator Antoine de La Garanderie (1920-2010) which was at its most popular in the 1990s, could be helpful in this case. Although mental management fell into obscurity for a time, it has been rediscovered in recent years.

Mental management is based on dialogue with an education professional and aims to illustrate the individual's cognitive habits. It is not about testing the individual, but rather about questioning them in order to build up their learning profile and in doing so allow them to understand themselves better.

Once they understand how their mind works, the person can start to learn the five mental processes that will make it easier to deal with their giftedness, namely attention, memorisation, comprehension, reflection and creativity. These concepts each have their own specific features, and involve:

- paying attention to the world around us;
- knowing how and why to memorise information;
- adding new knowledge to existing information;
- reflecting on what we have learned;
- inventing new things.

Mental management allows individuals to find out whether they are an auditory, visual or kinaesthetic learner and teaches them tools so that they can use all of these sensory channels and learn more effectively.

This method can also be useful for identifying learning methods that are not working and for teaching the individual new ways of learning, which they can then adopt and master.

Thanks to mental management, your child will know what methods help them to learn, use the right tools for them, define their goals more precisely and increase their independence.

IMPROVED SOCIAL RELATIONSHIPS

One of the key challenges of parenting a gifted child is helping them to develop a network of peers and work on their social relationships.

- Connecting with the people around them is not always easy for gifted children, as they may avoid their classmates and prefer talking to people who are older than them. There are a range of possible reasons for this: some hypersensitive children may experience bullying or mockery, while others may simply be fed up with justifying the behaviour that comes naturally to them. In some cases, depending on the child, their teacher and their class, it may be helpful for them to talk to their classmates (and not just their teachers) about their giftedness. In other cases, a brief explanation may be all that is needed if the other children ask questions or the adaptations that have been put in place for the gifted child are very noticeable. The teacher could also ask whether other pupils find a particular theory easier to understand when it has been explained as though for a gifted child, as this may also be beneficial to other students.

- These interpersonal difficulties should not be minimised. Be there for your child as much as you can if they are feeling lonely or finding it difficult to get on with other children. They should not have to suffer alone: even though they may not show it, your support will be invaluable to them.
- Rather than downplaying any problems or showing up at your child's school to try and resolve them yourself, listen to them, be empathetic and understanding, and suggest some ideas to improve their relationships with other people.
- Gifted children need to understand that other children's games can also be fun for them and improve their skills and strategic abilities. Spending time with other children their own age can also introduce them to other ways of seeing the world and enable them to fit in with their peers. This will help them throughout their life, as it will allow them to make friends,

have romantic relationships, work effectively with colleagues of a similar age, and so on.

- Once the child grasps this, they will realise that talking to or playing with other children will allow them to develop new skills and thrive. This does not mean that they cannot talk to their teachers or go read in the library from time to time: the aim is to find a balance that does not leave them isolated from their classmates. Make sure they know that they can make compromises, so that they sometimes do things by themselves and sometimes, when they feel up to it, play and interact with other children their age.
- Show them that they can also suggest games or things to talk about with other children. They do not have to keep all their ideas to themselves, as some of their classmates may share their enthusiasm. Of course, not everyone will necessarily want to be friends with your child – this is a normal part of all relationships! Being shut out of a group can happen to anyone, not just gifted children, so you should make it clear that their giftedness is not necessarily the reason some of their classmates do not want to be friends, or they

may end up struggling to accept this part of themselves.

- Your child needs to feel supported and to avoid isolating themselves. Ask them to look out for other children their age who are unusual in one way or another, as this will make them realise that they are not the only person who functions a little differently. When they talk to their classmates, they may find out that one of them collects figurines of fantasy characters, while another is having a hard time at home, which should reassure them about their own situation.
- If they are not getting on with some of their classmates, reassure them that they can always talk to a trusted adult and that things will get better in time.
- Explain that having a problem with one classmate does not mean that all children are like that and that they should automatically be on their guard. Show them that they can open up to other people, without unquestioningly putting their trust in everyone they meet.

<u>**SUMMARY**</u>

- Listen.
- Be empathetic.
- Offer some solutions, for example by helping them to fit in with a particular group.
- Show them that games can teach them things.
- Show them that plenty of other people are unusual in some way.
- Talk to them about adults that they can trust.
- Make sure they know that every situation is different and they do not have to mistrust other people.

EMOTIONAL WELLBEING

We all have rich emotional lives, and gifted children are no exception to this. As we have already explained, what makes gifted children different is the intensity of their feelings rather than the quantity. Sometimes, their emotions are so intense that they feel as though they are constantly under pressure. The following tips will help you to support your child as they develop a more nuanced understanding of what they are feeling.

Relaxing hobbies

As a general rule, you should suggest activities that allow them to interact with the world around them, and you should feel free to encourage hobbies that enable them to understand and express their emotions. These could include board games, puppetry, theatre, laughter yoga, art therapy, role playing, improv, dance and Biodanza (an approach which uses movement set to music to achieve greater emotional awareness), among other hobbies. From infancy onwards, you can find games focused on emotional development in shops for children.

Furthermore, other people tend to put pressure on gifted children to always perform at a high level, when they need time to relax and the opportunity to fail just like everyone else. Gifted individuals' lives are certainly not any easier than the lives of the rest of the population.

You can help your child to relax by giving them some time to focus on nothing but enjoying themselves, if that is what they want. For example, you could encourage them to spend time outside, or to try a more unusual activity such as laughter yoga. Participants in this group activity alternate between breathing exercises and forced laughter, which the brain responds to in the same way as real laughter, meaning that the person experiences the same benefits in terms of relaxation and wellbeing. Moreover, laughter yoga helps participants to feel more comfortable as part of a group and to deal with putting themselves in ridiculous situations (pulling funny faces) so that they can learn to laugh at themselves.

The idea is to allow your child to think about something other than their schoolwork and other activities where performance is important. Their only aim should be to work off excess energy and relax.

You may also want to suggest an activity that allows them to showcase and share what makes them different. Good options for gifted children are music, drawing and artistic activities in general, as long as they do not become too focused on performance. The aim should be to show them that their giftedness is a good thing and a source of enrichment for them rather than a burden in their everyday life.

Therapy

If your child is still anxious and tense in spite of your attempts to introduce relaxing hobbies, specific relaxation activities and sophrology (a collection of physical and mental activities used to boost health and wellbeing) are worth a try, and should be good first steps to giving your child some relief from the tension they are feeling.

Indeed, constantly trying to adapt themselves to the people around them can prove exhausting over the long term. These approaches will make it possible to treat the stress, anxiety, depression and other problems that are stopping your child from living in peace.

If your child is finding it difficult to adapt, feels as though all their social interactions end in failure, is too afraid to go to school, dreads breaktime or is falling behind in a number of subjects, therapy may be a good idea. Some psychologists specialise in giftedness, or are even gifted themselves.

While some gifted individuals want to work with a therapist who is also gifted, the most important thing is that your child feels comfortable with their therapist. If they do not, feel free to arrange meetings with other therapists until you find one that your child clicks with and with whom they can make good progress. It is therefore vital to consult your child about how they are feeling throughout the process.

Whatever therapy you arrange for your child, this is not a substitute for support from all their family members. They need to feel that you love them and are there for them every day. As far as possible, provide them with support and guidance which will help them to feel that they fit in at home and to be themselves, both within and outside their family.

You may also want to see a therapist if your child's difficulties are making you anxious. It is entirely normal to be worried about your child's future when they are struggling, or to be reminded of your own difficulties when you were younger. You may feel that your child's journey will be as difficult as yours was and end up smothering them with recommendations and advice that they do not really need.

EVERY CHILD IS DIFFERENT

Although there is a wealth of advice out there about dealing with a gifted child, you need to remember that every child is different. It is up to you to assess the situation and make the right decisions for you and your child.

Like with everything, outside influences can make us doubt ourselves. You need to be able to take a step back from the things you read and hear and consider your child's feelings and personality to know what is best for them.

Although you are the one who will have the final say about your child's education, it is still a good idea to regularly check in with them and ask them how they are doing without judgement, and to try and take an interest in what they are doing.

You can use the template below to record the worries, no matter how big or small, that your child might be experiencing on a daily basis, your approach to interacting with them, and any points that you would like to raise with their teachers.

You can come back to your notes regularly to see if there have been any improvements. Remember that the aim is not for the situation to be perfect, but to find a greater degree of balance.

Situations that have improved (for example, they have started working harder at school):

....

....

....

....

....

Situations that I am concerned about (for example, they never talk about their friends):

....

....

....

....

....

What is the best time to talk to my child about their giftedness (for example, Saturday evening, when they are relaxed)?

....

....

....

....

....

Things they have taken an interest in recently (for example, the theatre):

....

....

....

....

....

Feedback for their teacher the next time I see them (for example, that I appreciate their involvement):

....

....

....

....

....

ASSOCIATIONS FOR GIFTED CHILDREN

If you are struggling to find answers to any questions you might have, feel free to get in touch with one of the many specialised organisations for gifted children and their parents.

Associations for gifted individuals exist in many countries. In the UK, these include the National

Association for Able Children in Education (NACE) and Potential Plus UK (formerly known as the National Association for Gifted Children). Their websites are packed with information on giftedness and ways of supporting gifted children, and they also organise seminars and conferences on the topic.

It is also worth taking some time to look at the many blogs and forums devoted to gifted individuals and the problems they may experience. This will make you feel less alone, give you the opportunity to ask very precise questions and receive support from people who understand your situation, and pick up original ideas to guide your child through their everyday life.

FAQS

WHAT ARE THE STEPS TO GETTING MY CHILD OFFICIALLY CLASSIFIED AS GIFTED?

The first step is to identify multiple signs of giftedness in your child. A single characteristic is not enough, but several in combination should give you an indication that your child may be gifted.

Do not hesitate to discuss the matter with your child: do they feel as though they do not fit in with other people? Do they have the impression that they think differently from their family and friends? How do they perceive things? If you subsequently decide to seek confirmation from a specialist, take the time to explain to your child how it will work and what the point of it is.

Once you have made your decision, choose a psychologist who is qualified to carry out the tests. You can find contact details on the websites of associations for gifted children. If your child's school has a psychologist, they may be able to point you in the right direction, but they probably will not have the necessary expertise to organise the tests themselves.

WHAT TEACHING METHODS AND ALTERNATIVES TO SCHOOL ARE THERE FOR GIFTED CHILDREN?

This varies depending on your country. You should be able to find out what is available where you are by looking at the website of the ministry of education.

Here, you will find information about the accommodations that can be made for gifted children. Some schools use active teaching methods, which means that your child may be given additional projects to do or given the opportunity to satisfy their curiosity and explore certain subjects further.

As well as skipping a year, which is still a somewhat contentious issue, some schools teach students from multiple year groups together during primary school, so your child may be able to follow classes for different ages. They may also be able to start school before the usual age.

Other options are available, such as special schools in some countries, home schooling and more advanced examinations. However, some of these options risk making your child feel lonelier, as they will spend less time mixing with other children their age. It is up to you to decide if they are right for your child.

WHAT ARE THE SIGNS THAT A CHILD HAS HIGH INTELLECTUAL POTENTIAL?

There are many signs that can indicate that a child may be gifted, but they vary depending on the child's age. Indeed, the indicators that you should pay attention to in a 2-year-old will be different from those exhibited by a 6- or 8-year-old.

Some of these signs are linked to the child's attitude to learning, while other are more to do with their interpersonal relationships.

In terms of cognitive abilities, see if your child learns to read and speak quickly, if they take an interest in a wide range of subjects, if they learn independently and do not need to be pushed by a teacher to explore a particular topic in more detail, if they repeatedly ask existential questions, etc. However, remember that if your child is very curious, that does not automatically mean that they are gifted, as there are other factors to consider.

In terms of interpersonal relationships, see if your child is very empathetic, has a keen sense of justice and reacts strongly to a range of stimuli. They may also feel that they do not fit in with other children their age or that they think differently to other people.

DOES MY CHILD ABSOLUTELY REQUIRE PSYCHOLOGICAL SUPPORT?

It is strongly recommended that you seek confirmation that your child is gifted, as this will help them to feel understood and to better manage their giftedness.

However, you may still be wondering if there is more you need to be doing. It is worth observing whether your child struggles to fit in at home, at school and with other people in general, and whether they display any behavioural problems or signs of depression.

In these cases, if your child is struggling to deal with their giftedness, it is a good idea to consult a psychologist so that your child can deal with the tension they are feeling, recognise their strengths and better manage their relationships.

The need for a specialist to help your child deal with their giftedness on an everyday basis does not have to be a source of stress. It is not always easy to identify what is not working yourself or to confide in your friends and family, as you may be afraid that they will judge you. However, make sure that you listen to your child if they say that they do not get on with their psychologist, and do not be afraid to look for a different one.

ARE THE PARENTS AND SIBLINGS OF A GIFTED CHILD NECESSARILY GIFTED AS WELL?

Gifted children may also have gifted parents and siblings, but this is not necessarily the case. Even if multiple members of the family are gifted, they will probably have different experiences. For example, one child may be disruptive in class, while another is completely inhibited.

If you have other children who are not gifted, make sure that you do not let them feel that you value them less than your gifted child. They are not less intelligent; their minds just work differently.

Pay close attention to the relationships between your children and the things they complain about most frequently. This will allow you to step in more quickly in case of problems and avoid letting trivial matters come between them. Giftedness should not be seen as a curse or a source of conflict and tension, and finding the right balance will enable you to live in peace with it.

SHOULD I BE WORRIED IF MY CHILD ONLY SOCIALISES WITH OTHER GIFTED CHILDREN?

Gifted children often feel that they do not fit in with their peers, so it is understandable that they will be relieved to find other children who are like them and do not find their way of thinking strange.

Socialising exclusively with older people and other gifted children is only a cause for concern if their behaviour with non-gifted people really poses a problem. This behaviour may be a sign that they harbour misunderstandings, prejudices or even hatred after a painful event (bullying by non-gifted children, humiliation by a teacher, and so on).

That said, gifted children's behaviour towards their non-gifted peers is not necessarily rooted in hatred: they may struggle to accept themselves and be afraid that others will reject them. Above all, do not jump to conclusions! It is essential that you talk to your child about your worries and work out why they do not want to socialise with non-gifted children.

ARE GIFTED INDIVIDUALS MORE AT RISK OF DEPRESSION?

Giftedness does not inevitably lead to depression, but individuals are more at risk when they feel that they do not fit in with other people, have the impression that they are not being catered to at school, constantly find themselves pondering existential questions, or do not dare to really be themselves around others because they are afraid of rejection.

Depression can be mild, moderate or severe, but no matter the degree of severity, it is worth seeking psychological treatment. Never try to downplay your child's depression. Instead, do everything you can to support them and do some research about this illness to help you understand it better.

We want to hear from you!
Leave a comment on your online library
and share your favourite books on social media!

FURTHER READING

BIBLIOGRAPHY

- Bléandonu, G. (2004) *Les enfants intellectuellement précoces*. Paris: PUF.

- Fédération Wallonie-Bruxelles. (No date) *Hauts potentiels – espace 'tout public' – les aspects de la scolarité*. [Online]. [Accessed 8 December 2017]. Available from: <http://www.enseignement.be/index.php?page=25014>

- De Kermadec, M. (2015) *L'enfant précoce aujourd'hui. Le préparer au monde de demain*. Paris: Albin Michel.

- Maillard, C. (2007) *La gestion mentale, voyage au cœur des émotions*. Lyon: Chronique sociale.

- Papoutsaki, P. (2006) *Enfants surdoués, enfants créateurs ?* Paris: L'Harmattan.

- Revol, O., Poulin, R. and Perrodin, D. (2015) *100 idées pour accompagner les enfants à haut potentiel*. Paris: Tom Pousse.

- Vaineau, A-L. (2017) Enfant précoce, surdoué : faire de sa différence une richesse. *Psychologies*. [Online]. [Accessed 8 December 2017]. Available from: <http://www.psychologies.com/Famille/Enfants/Apprentissage/Articles-et-Dossiers/

<u>Enfant-precoce-surdoue-faire-de-sa-difference-une-richesse</u>>

ADDITIONAL SOURCES

- Distin, K. ed. (2006) *Gifted Children: A Guide for Parents and Professionals.* London: Jessica Kingsley Publishers.

- Freeman, J. (2010) *Gifted Lives: What Happens when Gifted Children Grow Up.* Abingdon: Routledge.

- Webb, J. T., Gore, J. L., Amend, E. R. and DeVries, A. R. (2007) *A Parent's Guide to Gifted Children.* Scottsdale, Arizona: Great Potential Press, Inc.

www.50minutes.com

Ebook EAN: 9782808006361

Paperback EAN: 9782808007313

Legal Deposit: D/2017/12603/940

Cover: © Primento

Digital conception by Primento, the digital partner of publishers.